Developing Positive Christian Character

by Roger Hillis

© 2018 One Stone Press.
All rights reserved. No part of this book may be reproduced in any form without written permission of the publisher.

Published by:
One Stone Press
979 Lovers Lane
Bowling Green, KY 42103

Printed in the United States of America

ISBN 13: 978-1-941422-40-3

www.onestone.com

Table of Contents

1. Faithfulness 5
2. Contentment 9
3. Courage 13
4. Integrity 17
5. Compassion 21
6. Moral Purity 25
7. Humility 29
8. Respect 33
9. Maturity 37
10. Kindness 41
11. Diligence 45
12. Perseverance 49

All scripture references, unless otherwise noted, are taken from the New King James Version, copyright by Thomas H. Nelson, Inc., Nashville, Tennessee, 1979, 1980, 1982, 1993. Used by permission.

Developing Positive Christian Character

Your reputation is what people think about you (Proverbs 22:1). It is what people see about your life. It is the example you set for others. It is important to be a good example and have a good reputation (Matthew 5:13-16).

On the other hand, your character is what you are on the inside. Character is who you really are. It is who you are when no one is looking. Timothy had consistently shown his "proven character" (Philippians 2:22, NKJV). Other versions (ESV and NASV for example) refer to this as "proven worth." It is the type of life you have regularly lived and it reveals, in the long term, your real value to the Lord.

Reputation is what people think you are. Character is what God knows you are.

Your character is a matter of choice, not of birth. You can become what you want to be. You can change parts of your character that are not what you want them to be.

If you do not treat others the way you should, you can change.

If you are not morally pure, you can be.

If your speech is improper, it can be different.

If you need an attitude adjustment, you can do that too.

Read 1 Samuel 16:7. As God looks at your heart, what does He see? Is He pleased? Is He saddened? Does He see someone who is trying to be like Christ, or someone who is living like the world?

Samuel picked David, a man after God's own heart. Does that phrase describe you? It could, if you decide you want that.

Will you resolve in your heart to do this? Will you be purer in heart? Will you develop and grow your character to be what God wants you to be? You can decide to do that right now. Will you?

Lesson 1

Faithfulness

"But the fruit of the Spirit is love, joy, peace, longsuffering, kindness, goodness, faithfulness, gentleness, self-control. Against such there is no law" (Galatians 5:22-23). One character quality that the apostle Paul describes as a fruit of the Spirit led life is faithfulness.

There are numerous synonyms for faithfulness, including reliability, dependability, and trustworthiness.

One who is faithful is a person you can always count on. He is determined to do what he says he will do. He does not make rash or irresponsible promises. He is a man of his word. Other factors may determine the outcome of the situation, but, if it is possible to fulfill his word, based on his will and actions, the job will get done.

To be faithful a person must be full of faith, like the seven men described in Acts 6:3-6. Given a task to perform for God, they will carry it out, to the very best of their ability. They will not give up, will not quit, will not grow weary in doing good things. They can be trusted. They are dependable. They are constant.

Many people are good at volunteering to do a work for God. Others are excellent at starting lots of activities. A faithful person is one who, motivated by his love for God and his fellowman, finishes the job.

Are you faithful? Can you be counted on? If a job needs to be done, are you dependable to do what you have promised to do? To develop a positive, Christian character, you need to be faithful.

> Therefore, brethren, seek out from among you seven men of **good reputation**, full of the Holy Spirit and wisdom, whom we may appoint over this business... and they chose Stephen, a man **full of faith** and the Holy Spirit, and Philip, Prochorus, Nicanor, Timon, Parmenas, and Nicolas, a proselyte from Antioch, whom they set before the apostles; and when they had prayed, they laid hands on them.
>
> - Acts 6:3-6

Philippians 2:19-30

Timothy (verses 19-24)

> But I trust in the Lord Jesus to send Timothy to you shortly... for I have no one like-minded, who will sincerely care for your state. For all seek their own, not the things which are of Christ Jesus. But you know his **proven character**...
>
> - Philippians 2:19-22

1. What was Timothy going to do for Paul (verse 19)? _____

2. Why was Timothy the one chosen to go to Philippi (verse 20)? _____

3. What was different about Timothy from others (verse 21)? _____

4. What is "proven character" (verse 22)? _____

5. How had Timothy proven his character to Paul? _____

Epaphroditus (verses 25-30)

> Receive [Epaphroditus] therefore in the Lord with all gladness, and **hold such men in esteem**...
>
> - Philippians 2:29-30

1. What five descriptions does Paul use of Epaphroditus (verse 25)? _____

2. Why was Epaphroditus "distressed" (verse 26)? _____

3. What does it mean to "hold such men in esteem" (verse 29)? _____

4. How had Epaphroditus shown his faithfulness (verse 30)? _____

The Little Things

"The kingdom of heaven is like a mustard seed, which a man took and sowed in his field, which indeed is the least of all the seeds; but when it is grown it is greater than the herbs and becomes a tree, so that the birds of the air come and nest in its branches" (Matthew 13:31-32).

Jesus used this parable to illustrate that great things in the kingdom of God can result from faithfulness in the little things that we all do. Here are some "little things" that we all can do.

- Help a sick neighbor
- Give someone a ride to the doctor
- Show kindness to a brother or sister
- Speak hope to the lost
- Hand a Bible tract to someone
- Write a short letter to one who needs encouragement
- Invite someone to services
- Pray for the weak
- Call one who is lonely
- Visit a shut-in
- Buy someone some groceries
- Pray for the elders, deacons and preachers
- Cry with someone who is hurting

The little things are the easiest to do and are often the most appreciated. But things that are the easiest to do are also the easiest to overlook. Do yourself and someone else a favor today. Be faithful to reach out with the little things and watch for great results.

"He who is faithful in what is least is faithful also in much; and he who is unjust is what is least is unjust also in much" (Luke 16:10).

Total Commitment

A lack of commitment explains the indifference so common among many Christians today. How many members of an average congregation are actively involved in soul winning? Are members more spiritually minded or worldly minded? Are our families centered around spiritual activities? Do we have proper relationships with our brothers and sisters in Christ? How many members are truly devoted to daily Bible study and prayer? Are lukewarm Christians really faithful? Are they really going to heaven? The problem is a lack of commitment to Jesus Christ.

"I have been crucified with Christ; it is no longer I who live, but Christ lives in me; and the life which I now live in the flesh I live by faith in the Son of God, who loved me and gave Himself for me" (Galatians 2:20).

Examples of Faithfulness

Young People

- Meeting deadlines
- Cleaning your room without being told
- Getting your homework done
- Taking care of a pet
- Arriving home on time
- Studying a Bible lesson for class
- Keeping your life pure

Adults

- Promising to complete a job around the house
- Parents putting their children's needs before their own
- Helping needy people who can't pay you back
- A wife caring for an invalid husband
- Husbands and wives committing purity only to one another
- An employee on the job being a hard worker
- Becoming a Christian and never looking back (Revelation 2:10)

Can you think of three more examples (appropriate for your age group)?

1. _____
2. _____
3. _____

Contentment

In the first century the apostle Paul wrote, in Philippians 4:11-12, that he had learned "the secret of being content" (NIV). However, in our generation, contentment is a "secret" that many people have yet to learn.

Much of our discontent comes from a desire to have more physical possessions. Although we are, for the most part, an extremely blessed people, many of us dream of having even more and more "things." For that reason, the Bible warns us repeatedly against covetousness, greed and a desire to be rich. It is written that "the love of money" is the root of all evil (1 Timothy 6:10).

Covetousness is a sin that is easier to see in others than it is to recognize in ourselves. It is a deceptive evil and one of Satan's most effective weapons against disciples of Christ.

Ephesians 5:5 goes so far as to tell us that covetousness is one form of idolatry, something that can replace the worship of God. All too often, the love of money is greater than the love of God in our hearts. Jesus firmly states that it is impossible to serve both God and mammon (possessions) then challenges us to choose between the two (Matthew 6:24).

Contentment is a matter of one's attitude and character. It is easier to talk about this subject than it is to live out God's will in our daily lives.

Proverbs About Money

What does each of these verses teach us about our attitude toward money and possessions?

11:4 _____
_____

Steps to Contentment

(Discuss each of these points as you have time)

1. Learn to live within your means.
2. Make a budget and stick with it. Self-discipline will be required.
3. Distinguish between wants and needs.
4. Have the proper attitude toward possessions.

Sayings of Jesus About Money

Read these passages and list the main point Christ made about contentment or covetousness.

- Matthew 6:19-21 _____
- Mark 4:18-19 _____
- Mark 10:23 _____
- Luke 12:15 _____
- Luke 16:13-14 _____

11:28 _____

13:7 _____

23:4-5 _____

28:11 _____

30:8-9 _____

Ecclesiastes 5:10-12

1. What does it mean to love silver? _____

2. What is abundance? _____

3. Why did the writer say "this also is vanity?" _____

4. What does verse 11 teach us? _____

5. Why does a rich person often have trouble sleeping? _____

The Epistles

It is not only Proverbs and the gospels that deal with our attitude toward money. The rest of the

LESSON 2 Contentment

New Testament also has much to say about the subject. What can we learn from each of these verses?

Philippians 4:11-12 _____

1 Timothy 6:6-10 _____

1 Timothy 6:17-19 _____

Hebrews 13:5 _____

Revelation 3:17 _____

New Testament Examples of Covetousness

How do these people illustrate this lesson?

Rich, young ruler (Matthew 19:16-22) _____

Rich farmer (Luke 12:16-21) _____

Felix (Acts 24:26) _____

Judas Iscariot (Matthew 26:14-16) _____

Conclusion

There may well be more warnings in the Bible against covetousness and greed than any other single sin. Every kind of evil can spring forth from a greedy heart. Please examine your own attitude toward money. Covetousness is a very serious sin. Do not lose your soul over money.

Lesson 3

Courage

"Finally, my brethren, be strong in the Lord and in the power of His might" (Ephesians 6:10).

Courage is bravery, a willingness to face a difficult situation head-on without flinching.

Courage is boldness, an attitude that overcomes opposition, no matter how intense or unrelenting it may be.

Courage is not the absence of fear, but rather it is doing what needs to be done in spite of one's fear.

Courage is a character quality of one who does not let other intimidate him or push him around. It describes one who is God's man or God's woman and does what is right in hard or challenging conditions.

The key to being courageous is found in a desire to please God. "For do I now persuade men, or God? Or do I seek to please men? For if I still pleased men, I would not be a bondservant of Christ" (Galatians 1:10). There can be circumstances when both are possible. (My children please me when they obey God and that pleases Him also.)

But when a difficult choice has to be made, a person of courage makes the right decision and, regardless of what other people may think, does what is right in the sight of God.

"Wait on the LORD; Be of good courage, And He shall strengthen your heart; Wait, I say, on the LORD!" (Psalm 27:14).

Comment on and discuss these sayings about courage:

"Never run away from anything. Never!"
—Winston Churchill

"Courage is resistance to fear, mastery of fear— not absence of fear."
—Mark Twain

"The greatest test of courage on earth is to bear defeat without losing heart."
—Robert Green Ingersoll

"Courage is grace under pressure."
—Ernest Hemingway

"A ship in harbor is safe, but that is not what ships are built for."
—William Shedd

> Have I not commanded you? **Be strong and of good courage**; do not be afraid, nor be dismayed, for the Lord your God is with you wherever you go.
>
> - Joshua 1:9

Bible Examples

Joshua (Joshua 1:1-9)

1. What was Joshua's job? _____

2. How many times did God tell Joshua to be courageous? List the verses. _____

3. What was the key to Joshua's success? _____

4. Who told Joshua to be courageous in verse 18? _____

5. What was the military strategy against Jericho (6:1-5)? _____

6. Why did that strategy take courage? _____

Esther

1. Who was Esther? _____

2. Why would Mordecai not bow to Haman (Esther 3:2-5)? _____

3. What was Haman's plan for the Jews (3:6)? _____

LESSON 3 Courage

4. What does it mean that Esther had "come to the kingdom for such a time as this" (4:14)? _____ _____

5. How did Esther show tremendous courage (4:11, 16)? _____ _____

John the Baptist (Matthew 14:1-12)

1. What had John said that required great courage? _____ _____

2. What happened to John because he told the truth? _____ _____

3. Was there some other way he might have approached the situation and saved his life? _____ _____

4. Would you be willing to die if you told the truth or would you be tempted to lie? _____ _____

Stephen (Acts 7)

1. What had Stephen said that made the crowd so hostile (verses 51-52)? _____ _____

2. What was the crowd's first reaction (verse 54)? _____ _____

> And so I will go to the king, which is against the law; and **if I perish, I perish!**
>
> - Esther 4:16

3. What was their second response (verses 57-59)? _____
   _____

4. Why didn't Stephen soften the message? _____
   _____

Three Final Questions

1. Can you think of any other Bible examples of courage? _____
   _____
   _____

2. Can you think of some non-biblical examples of courage? _____
   _____
   _____

3. Can you tell of one instance in your own life when you have shown courage? _____
   _____

Lesson 4

Integrity

"Let integrity and uprightness preserve me, For I wait for You" (Psalm 25:21).

What comes to your mind when you hear the word integrity?

Maybe you think of honesty. A person of integrity is a person who is always honest in his words and actions. Truth is of utmost importance to him. He is one who "swears to his own hurt and does not change" (Psalm 15:4). He will not go back on his word. His yes means yes and his no always means no (Matthew 5:37).

Abraham Lincoln said, "No man has a good enough memory to make a successful liar."

Thomas Jefferson said, "Honesty is the first chapter of the book of wisdom."

King Solomon said, "The truthful lip shall be established forever, But a lying tongue is but for a moment" (Proverbs 12:19).

Perhaps the word "integrity" makes you think of moral purity. It describes someone who wants to live right. He desires to be a godly example before others and so, he seeks to live a consistent, holy life. He can be trusted with money, with power, with knowledge of another's failures. He will not gossip, will not behave in an unseemly manner, and will not seek to hurt others in any way.

Or maybe you think of "security." A person of integrity will not crumble under pressure, will not give up under relentless persecution, and will not be tossed about by the winds of public opinion. He

Sayings About Honesty

What is your response to these sayings?

"A lie may take care of the present, but it has no future."

"Beware of the half truth. You may have gotten hold of the wrong half."

"Truthfulness is essential among friends. A person who does not tell the truth is not your friend."

"Integrity is the essence of everything successful."
—Chinese fortune cookie

is rock solid and true. He is dependable and always trustworthy.

To develop positive, Christian character, a disciple of Christ must be a person of integrity. "He who walks with integrity walks securely..." (Proverbs 10:9).

Acts 5:1-11 – Ananias and Sapphira

1. How does this passage show how much God hates lying? _____
   _____

2. What was their lie? _____
   _____

3. In what sense were they testing the Lord (verse 9)?
   _____
   _____

Different Kinds of Lies

For each of these, explain what this type of lie includes and list some current day examples.

1. Half truth (Genesis 12:11-13)_____
   _____
   _____
   _____

2. Exaggeration (Exodus 32:22-24)_____
   _____
   _____
   _____

3. Afraid to tell the truth (Matthew 26:69-74)
   _____
   _____

Examples of Dishonesty

- Cheating—looking on someone else's paper
- Stealing—taking too much change at the store
- Not paying your debts
- Lying to your parents (or children), teachers, friends, spouse, etc.

What are some other examples of dishonesty?

_____
_____
_____
_____
_____
_____

4. Deceit (Mark 7:22) _____
   _____
   _____

5. Religious deception (2 Corinthians 11:13-15) _____
   _____
   _____

Proverbs About Truth and Lying

Read these proverbs and comment on them as they apply to this study.

- 10:2 _____
  _____

- 11:1 _____
  _____

- 12:17-22 _____
  _____

- 13:11 _____
  _____

- 20:7 _____
  _____

- 20:14 _____
  _____

Write out Revelation 21:8 in the space below. Read it carefully and thoughtfully. What does it teach us about how God feels about lying and how serious He considers it to be?

_____
_____
_____
_____

Lesson 5

Compassion

One of the important qualities found in a person of character is compassion, caring about other people and their needs.

"Let nothing be done through selfish ambition or conceit, but in lowliness of mind let each esteem others better than himself. Let each of you look out not only for his own interests, but also for the interests of others" (Philippians 2:3-4).

A compassionate person is not selfish, but rather is willing to sacrifice personally to help others. And he is not concerned about the praise or credit he may receive from helping. His only motivation is to do what is best for another.

The word, compassion, means "to feel with." If the other person is suffering, he hurts also. If he is lonely, the compassionate person is there to meet that need. A compassionate person rejoices with those who rejoice and weeps with those who weep (Romans 12:15).

Another term that describes this character quality is the Greek word, *agape*. Translated as "love" in most (maybe all?) of the newer versions, the old King James Version attempted to distinguish between the various Greek terms by rendering agape as "charity." While that might not be the best word to use in today's society, it does carry with it the idea of helping others who can't help themselves and doing so because you care about them.

Compassion can be shown in many ways. It might be through a gift, a hug, by spending time with someone or simply through lending an ear.

> But whoever has this world's goods, and **sees his brother in need**, and shuts up his heart from him, how does the love of God abide in him?
>
> - 1 John 3:17

> But do not forget **to do good and to share**, for with such sacrifices God is well pleased.
>
> - Hebrews 13:16

Are You Selfish or Unselfish?

A selfish person thinks only of himself. An unselfish person thinks of ways he (or she) can help others. What do these verses teach us about helping other people?

- Mark 10:44 _____ _____

- Romans 15:1-2 _____ _____

- Galatians 6:1 _____ _____

- Galatians 6:2 _____ _____

- Galatians 6:10 _____ _____

- Hebrews 13:16 _____ _____

- James 2:15-17 _____ _____

- 1 John 3:17 _____ _____

Anything that shows love and concern for others is an act of compassion.

Luke 10:30-37

Notice that there are four different kinds of people represented in the parable of the Good Samaritan.

Lonely People

1. Who is the lonely person in this parable? _____

2. Who are some modern day examples of this type of person? _____

Cruel People

1. Who are the cruel people in this parable? _____

2. Who are some modern day examples of this type of person? _____

Selfish People

1. Who are the selfish people in this parable? _____

2. Who are some modern day examples of this type of person? _____

Compassionate People

1. Who is the compassionate person in this parable? _____

LESSON 5 Compassion

2. What are some of the differences between the Samaritan and the injured man? _____
_____
_____

3. Who are some modern day examples of this type of person? _____
_____

4. What do Christ's final words in this setting mean to you and your life? _____
_____
_____

Barnabas

His original name was Joses (or Joseph). It means "May God help." The apostles changed his name to Barnabas, which means "the Son of Encouragement." Read the passages below and tell whom he helped and how.

Acts 4:32-37 _____
_____
_____

Acts 9:27 _____
_____
_____

Acts 11:22-26 _____
_____
_____

Acts 15:36-39 _____
_____
_____

Philippians 2:3-4

What are some specific ways that you show compassion by helping others? Maybe your family, your friends, your co-workers?

- _____
  _____
  _____

- _____
  _____
  _____

- _____
  _____
  _____

- _____
  _____
  _____

- _____
  _____
  _____

- _____
  _____
  _____

- _____
  _____
  _____

- _____
  _____
  _____

Lesson 6

Moral Purity

Christians are to keep themselves morally pure. "Pure and undefiled religion before God and the Father is this: to visit orphans and widows in their trouble, and to keep oneself unspotted from the world" (James 1:27). This passage starts with the word "pure" and ends with the phrase "unspotted from the world."

This is one of the areas of our lives in which we are to be radically different from the world. The distinction should be so clear and so obvious to non-Christians that there is no question we belong to the Lord.

Sometimes when we think about the difference between the church and the world, we focus on doctrinal purity, which is important. But the emphasis in the Bible has to do with how we personally live our lives. There is not to be a "hint of immorality" (Ephesians 5:3, NIV) in our lives as disciples of Christ.

It is all too easy for us to be influenced by the world in slow, often subtle ways. Satan entices us to take small steps away from purity, rather than huge jumps, but either way, we gradually find ourselves far afield from the biblical standards of holy conduct.

There are many synonyms for moral purity, including righteousness, holiness, godliness, sanctification, and virtue.

"Do not lay hands on anyone hastily, nor share in other people's sins; keep yourself pure" (1 Timothy 5:22).

> **Flee also youthful lusts**; but pursue righteousness, faith, love, peace with those who call on the Lord out of a **pure heart**.
> - 2 Timothy 2:22

> But put on the Lord Jesus Christ, and **make no provision for the flesh**, to fulfill its lusts.
> - Romans 13:14

"Let no one despise your youth, but be an example to the believers in word, in conduct, in love, in spirit, in faith, in purity" (1 Timothy 4:12).

Moral purity in life comes from moral purity in heart (Matthew 5:8).

Two Key Scriptures

2 Timothy 2:22

1. What are some examples of "youthful lusts?" _____

2. What does it mean to "flee" these things? _____

3. Why should followers of Christ pursue righteousness, faith, love, and peace? _____

4. What is the relationship between these positive things and calling on the Lord "out of a pure heart?" _____

Ephesians 5:3-7

1. Define these words listing various forms of impurity:

    Fornication_____

    Uncleanness_____

    Covetousness_____

You Have a Personal Choice

Be honest with yourself as you answer these two questions.

1. Are you different morally from your friends in the world? _____

2. What do you need to change about your life or your habits or your thoughts to be more pure?
_____
_____
_____
_____
_____

LESSON 6 Moral Purity

Filthiness _____

Foolish talking _____

Coarse jesting _____

Joseph and Purity (Genesis 39:1-20)

1. Approximately how old do you think Joseph was by this time? _____

2. Who would ever have known if Joseph had lain with Mrs. Potiphar? _____

3. How does verse 9 describe why Joseph refused her advances? _____

4. This account ends with Joseph in jail. What does that teach us about the consequences of doing the right thing? _____

5. What do we learn from verse 5? _____

Romans 13:13-14

1. What does it mean to walk properly, as in the day? _____

2. What is involved in making "no provision" for the flesh? _____

List specific examples of things people do that compromise their moral purity.

- _____
- _____
- _____
- _____
- _____
- _____
- _____

28 Developing Positive Christian Character

Define these words and find at least one verse where each is found.

Holiness _____
_____

Godliness_____
_____

Sanctification_____
_____

Virtue_____
_____

Lesson 7

Humility

Humility means not being conceited. It involves esteeming others first, above and before oneself. It includes looking out for the interests of others. It is the opposite of pride, arrogance, and self-righteousness.

"Let nothing be done through selfish ambition or conceit, but in lowliness of mind let each esteem others better than himself. Let each of you look out not only for his own interests, but also for the interests of others" (Philippians 2:3-4).

- One who is humble is not stubborn.
- One who is humble does not constantly think himself to be better than others.
- One who is humble does not believe that his or her ideas are always best.
- One who is humble is not afraid to admit when he is wrong.

Humility is not thinking you are worthless. Biblical teaching on humility, meekness, patience and love has led some to be convinced that they should be doormats for others. We are all created in the image of God with an immortal soul. Christ died for all people. You are valuable and matter to God and His people.

We are told not to think of ourselves more highly than we ought (Romans 12:3). The tax collector in the parable of Jesus (Luke 18-9-14) is an excellent example of humility while the Pharisee illustrates arrogance and self-righteousness.

"Likewise you younger people, submit yourselves to your elders. Yes, all of you be submissive to one

> For I say, through the grace given to me, to everyone who is among you, **not to think of himself more highly than he ought to think**, but to think soberly, as God has dealt to each one a measure of faith.
>
> - Romans 12:3

another; and be clothed with humility, for God resists the proud, but gives grace to the humble. Therefore humble yourselves under the mighty hand of God, that He may exalt you in due time" (1 Peter 5:5-6).

The Banquet Feast (Luke 14:7-11)

1. Why would people choose "the best places?" _____

2. What did Jesus say they should choose? _____

3. Why is it true that one who exalts himself will be humbled? _____

4. What does Jesus tell us to do in verse 12? _____

5. So have you ever done what Jesus says to do in a similar situation? _____

The Pharisee and the Tax Collector (Luke 18:9-14)

1. To whom did the Lord speak this parable? _____

2. Who were the Pharisees? _____

3. Who were the tax collectors? _____

4. How did the Pharisee pray wrong? _____

Results of Pride

What are some of the results of being filled with pride?

_____
_____
_____
_____
_____
_____
_____
_____

5. How did the tax collector pray right? _____
_____

Pride in Proverbs

Explain some of the times in your life when you may have seen these proverbs come true:

6:16-17 _____
_____

8:13 _____
_____

11:2 _____
_____

13:10 _____
_____

14:3 _____
_____

15:25 _____
_____

15:33 _____
_____

16:5 _____
_____

16:18 _____
_____

16:19 _____
_____

18:12 _____
_____

Results of Humility

What are some of the results of being a person of humility?

_____
_____
_____
_____
_____
_____
_____
_____
_____
_____
_____

21:24 _____
_____

22:4 _____
_____

25:6-7 _____
_____

28:25 _____
_____

29:23 _____
_____

One Special Note: Modesty

A huge problem in today's society is the prevalence of immodesty. Read 1 Timothy 2:9-10. How does this text connect modesty and humility?

_____
_____
_____

Lesson 8

Respect

Respect for others is a character quality that seems to be lacking in much of our modern society. Let's study together what the Bible says about respect.

To show respect means to think about, speak about and act toward others in a way that shows them honor and esteem. It includes having a high regard for people. It is often shown by acting in a courteous manner toward other people.

Children need to be taught respect in the home. Children who grow up with the proper respect for their parents will also learn to respect civil law, their teachers and administrators at school, and their superiors on the job.

Young people must be shown the proper respect for the rights and property of others.

In this way, young people learn to respect their elders and, ultimately, God.

"Children, obey your parents in the Lord, for this is right. Honor your father and mother, which is the first commandment with promise, that it may be well with you and you may live long on the earth" (Ephesians 6:1-3).

This is the kind of person that the book of Proverbs refers to as "wise."

One who does not show the proper respect for others is called a "fool."

Some of these things can be taught by words. Others are best shown by a godly example.

> You shall rise before the gray headed and **honor** the presence of an old man, and fear your God: I am the Lord.
> - Leviticus 19:32

> **Honor** all people.
> Love the brotherhood.
> Fear God.
> Honor the king.
> - 1 Peter 2:17

> Likewise you younger people, **submit** yourselves to your elders. Yes, all of you be submissive to one another, and **be clothed with humility**, for "God resists the proud, But gives grace to the humble."
> - 1 Peter 5:5

You and Your Parents (Ephesians 6:1-3)

1. How do you show respect or honor for your parents? _____

2. Is there a difference between respecting them as your parents and respecting their actions? _____

3. If you have (or had) lousy parents, does that mean you don't have to show them any respect? Explain your answer. _____

4. If you disagree with your parents, how should you handle that? _____

5. How do you think (at this point in your life) disrespectful children should be disciplined? _____

6. What do you think about the use of spanking to teach younger children to respect their parents and others? _____

7. The Old Testament says, "And he who curses his father or his mother shall surely be put to death" (Exodus 21:17). How long would you have lasted under that law? _____

LESSON 8 Respect 35

You, Your Parents and Proverbs

Read these verses from the book of Proverbs. Do these passages challenge you to change your relationship with your parents in any way?

10:1 _____

_____

13:1 _____

_____

15:5 _____

_____

15:20 _____

_____

19:26-27 _____

_____

20:20 _____

_____

23:22 _____

_____

23:24-25 _____

_____

Government Officials (Romans 13:1-7; 1 Peter 2:17)

1. Who would be included in these passages?
   _____
   _____

2. How would you show respect to these people?
   _____
   _____

What are some ways of showing disrespect for others?

_____
_____
_____
_____
_____
_____
_____
_____
_____
_____
_____
_____

Elders of the Church (1 Thessalonians 5:12-13; 1 Timothy 5:17-18)

1. Why is it important to respect the elders of the church? _____
   _____

2. What does "double honor" refer to? _____
   _____

3. How should you handle a disagreement with the elders? _____
   _____
   _____

The Elderly

1. What do these verses teach us about the respect we should all have for those who are older in age and/or in the faith?
   Leviticus 19:32 _____
   _____

   2 Chronicles 10:8 _____
   _____

   Job 12:12 _____
   _____

   Proverbs 16:31 _____
   _____

   1 Peter 5:5 _____
   _____

2. How would you summarize the attitude that you should have toward the elderly? _____
   _____

Lesson 9

Maturity

"When I was a child, I spoke as a child, I understood as a child, I thought as a child; but when I became a man, I put away childish things" (1 Corinthians 13:11).

What a simple illustration to represent spiritual growth. Once again taking something that is easily understood by everyone (a child growing into adulthood), the Lord helps us realize our goal is to grow and mature in the spiritual realm.

One chapter later, he says it this way: "Brethren, do not be children in understanding; however, in malice, be babes, but in understanding be mature" (1 Corinthians 14:20). In our attitudes toward others and God, we are to be "like little children" (Matthew 18:1-5). But in our spiritual development, we are to leave immaturity behind and draw closer and closer to God.

Maturity, then, carries with it the idea of spiritual progress. And at the heart of all spiritual growth is the concept of becoming more like our Master, Jesus Christ.

The Bible goes so far as to describe our spiritual maturity in terms of perfection. "Him we preach, warning every man and teaching every man in all wisdom, that we may present every man perfect in Christ Jesus" (Colossians 1:28).

When the Bible says that Christians should be perfect, we are always quick to note that this doesn't mean sinless perfection. But shouldn't that be our goal? Shouldn't we try to avoid sin at all cost? It is true that we will fall short (Romans 3:23), but shouldn't we do our very best to strive for perfection? It is all too easy to excuse intentional

> ...till we all come to the unity of the faith and of the knowledge of the Son of God, **to a perfect man**, to the measure of the stature of the fullness of Christ; that we should **no longer be children**...
>
> - Ephesians 4:13-14

sin in our lives by saying, "Well, nobody's perfect." True enough, but that is not an acceptable reason for us to quit trying to be perfect. That is what the Lord wants from us.

Time in the word (1 Peter 2:2) is the key to spiritual growth and maturity. That's why we should do our best to attend every assembly and every Bible class we can, to learn God's will and seek to put it into our lives daily. One step at a time, one day at a time, we grow into the image of God's Son (2 Corinthians 3:18).

Self-Examination Time

Paul said, "When I became a man, I put away childish things." Is there something in your life you need to put away to be more spiritually mature? Be honest.

_____
_____
_____
_____
_____
_____

Walking in His Footsteps (1 Peter 2:19-25)

1. What does it mean to "follow His steps?" _____
   _____

2. What does the word "example" mean? _____
   _____

3. What are some of the ways we should follow the example of Jesus? _____
   _____

4. How do these verses describe spiritual growth and maturity?

   Galatians 2:20 _____
   _____

   Galatians 4:19 _____
   _____

   Ephesians 4:13-14 _____
   _____

   Colossians 1:28 _____
   _____

   1 Timothy 4:15-16 _____
   _____

1 John 2:6 _____
_____

On to Maturity (Hebrews 5:12-6:3)

1. Why did the writer think they should be able to teach others? _____
_____

2. What is milk and what is solid food? _____
_____

3. What is meant by the phrase "by reason of use?" _____
_____

4. What does it mean to discern good and evil? _____
_____

Colossians 2:6-10

1. What does it mean to "walk in Him?" _____
_____

2. What does it mean to be "rooted and built up in Him and established in the faith?" _____
_____

3. How can we "beware" that the things in verse 8 don't happen to us? _____
_____

Those Immature Corinthians (1 Corinthians 3:1-3; 2 Corinthians 12:20)

Define these terms used by Paul that indicate immaturity.

Carnal _____
_____

From what we have talked about so far in this class, what "character quality" do you most need to grow in?

_____
_____
_____
_____

Envy _____
_____

Strife _____
_____

Divisions _____
_____

Contentions _____
_____

Jealousies _____
_____

Outbursts of wrath _____
_____

Selfish ambition _____
_____

Backbitings _____
_____

Whisperings _____
_____

Conceits _____
_____

Tumults _____
_____

Lesson 10

Kindness

The primary lesson from Christ's parable of the Good Samaritan (Luke 10:30-37) is that the Lord wants us to be kind, considerate, and helpful people.

It is God's desire for Christians to be described by such terms as "nice" and "kind." We should be obedient and polite, not ugly. Christians should do nice things for other people and not just think about themselves.

A person who is kind always speaks gently to others, not harshly.

You have probably heard of those who practice what they call, "random acts of kindness." What a terrific idea that greatly improves our world. Because kindness begets kindness, everyone would end up treating each other better. It would raise the level of society and, in the church, could encourage even more people to become Christians.

When Paul described love in 1 Corinthians 13, he wrote that "Love suffers long and is kind." People who love their neighbors as themselves (Mark 12:31) are, by their very nature, kind people. This kindness would include generosity and giving. It involves gentleness and goodness.

In Matthew 11:29, Jesus is described as "gentle and lowly in heart." Jesus was kind and gentle, patient with those who loved God and wanted to do right.

Kindness has many opposites—selfishness, harshness, stinginess, rudeness, arrogance, being inconsiderate, unthoughtfulness.

If people were to describe you in a single word, would those who know you best use the word, kind?

And **be kind** to one another, tenderhearted, forgiving one another, even as God in Christ forgave you.

- Ephesians 4:32

Therefore, as the elect of God, holy and beloved, put on tender mercies, **kindness**, humility, meekness, longsuffering...

- Colossians 3:12

A Couple of Bible Examples

How were these people's lives changed by kindness?

Genesis 24; especially verses 10-20

_____
_____
_____
_____
_____
_____
_____

2 Kings 4:8-17

_____
_____
_____
_____
_____

Ephesians 4:31-32

1. What negative qualities/attitudes should we eliminate? _____
_____
_____

2. What does it mean to be tenderhearted?
_____
_____

3. What is the final reminder in this passage?
_____
_____

Colossians 3:12-14

1. Which of these qualities (verses 12-13) is your biggest weakness? _____
_____

2. Which of these qualities is your greatest strength? _____
_____

3. Why is love called "the bond of perfection?"
_____
_____

Sayings About Kindness

What is your reaction or response to each of these sayings about being kind?

"You cannot do a kindness too soon, for you never know how soon it will be too late." (Ralph Waldo Emerson) _____
_____

LESSON 10 Kindness

"I can live for two months on a good compliment." (Mark Twain) _____
_____

"Kindness is the ability to love people more than they deserve." (Anonymous) _____
_____

"Kindness makes a fellow feel good whether it's being done to him or by him." (Frank A. Clark)
_____
_____

"Kindness has converted more sinners than zeal, eloquence, or learning." (Frederick W. Faber) _____
_____

"Kindness is more than deeds. It is an attitude, an expression, a look, a touch. It is anything that lifts another person." (C. Neil Strait)_____
_____

Bullying

One of society's biggest problems in the last few years is bullying.

1. Why is bullying so prevalent these days? _____
   _____

2. Is there a difference between bullying and teasing? _____

3. Have you ever been bullied yourself? How did that make you feel? _____
   _____

4. Looking back at your life, have you ever bullied another person?_____

Miscellaneous Thoughts and Verses about Kindness

What do we learn about kindness from these passages?

1 Peter 3:8

_____
_____
_____

Galatians 5:22

_____
_____
_____

Ephesians 2:7

_____
_____
_____

Acts 27:3

_____
_____
_____

Lesson 11

Diligence

Personal initiative is what the Bible refers to as "diligence."

One of the hardest things to teach people is to be self-motivated. For some reason, we often need to be pushed, nudged or otherwise encouraged to get on with what we know to be right.

There are many examples from everyday life.

- If you don't ever mow your yard, it will look terrible.
- If you don't change the oil in your car, it will burn up the engine.
- If you never take a bath or shower, you will run off all your friends.
- If you don't brush your teeth, they will eventually go away.

Who tells you to do these things?

One of the differences between a good student and an average one is often the initiative to study on his own.

Spiritually, we often "get after" Christians to work for God. Why is that necessary? It is because we often fail to take personal initiative.

We are taught to be diligent in our lives (2 Timothy 2:15). The NIV renders that as "do your best." Does that describe you? If not, are you willing to change so it does?

For a person of diligence and excellence, "average" is unacceptable. Something that is just good enough to pass is just not good enough. We are to be diligent in all that we do.

> Be **diligent** to present yourself approved to God, a worker who does not need to be ashamed, rightly dividing the word of truth.
>
> - 2 Timothy 2:15

A Few More Verses

Read these passages and comment on how they apply to serving God with diligence.

Matthew 20:1-16

_____

_____

_____

_____

Hebrews 4:9-11

_____

_____

_____

James 2:14-26

_____

_____

_____

John 9:4

_____

_____

_____

Laziness

The opposite of diligence is laziness and the opposite of a diligent person is one the Bible refers to as a "sluggard" or as one who is "slothful."

Read the following passages from the book of Proverbs and list how each one describes a lazy person.

10:4-5 _____

_____

13:4 _____

_____

15:19 _____

_____

18:9 _____

_____

20:4 _____

_____

21:25-26 _____

_____

24:30-34 _____

_____

26:13 _____

_____

26:14 _____

_____

26:15 _____

_____

26:16 _____

_____

The Parable of the Talents (Matthew 25:14-30)

1. In this parable, what is a talent? _____

2. How were the talents distributed? _____

3. What happened to those who used their talents properly? _____

4. What happened to the one who didn't diligently use his talent? _____

5. What talents do you think God has given you? Be honest about this. _____

6. Are you using the abilities that God gave you faithfully, diligently? Be honest here also. _____

Always Abounding

"Therefore, my beloved brethren, be steadfast, immovable, always abounding in the work of the Lord, knowing that your labor is not in vain in the Lord" (1 Corinthians 15:58).

The word "abounding" is from the same root word as abundant. Our service to the Lord is to be overflowing and free. It is not to be done grudgingly, sparingly, or cheaply. What are some examples of "always abounding" in the work of the Lord?

> I **must work** the works of Him who sent Me while it is day; the night is coming when no one can work.
>
> - John 9:4

> Let us therefore be **diligent** to enter that rest, lest anyone fall according to the same example of disobedience.
>
> - Hebrews 4:11

Giving freely and liberally of our possessions

When we understand that "The earth is the LORD'S and all its fullness" (Psalm 24:1), we see ourselves as simple stewards of our possessions. We must use all of our material blessings in the Lord's service. Giving into the collection plate is one way of doing that (1 Corinthians 16:1-2). Helping others who are in need is another (Galatians 6:10; James 1:27). Are you abounding in this great work?

Reaching out to the lost

As "fishers of men" (Mark 1:17), we must do all we can to help seek and save the lost. Someone has described evangelism as one beggar telling another beggar where to find bread. We have been saved to save others. This is an area of grave weakness in the church and we must do better. Many are not participating at all, let alone abounding in this work.

Practicing hospitality

Christians today just don't seem to spend as much time with one another as the first century Christians did. (That's an overstatement; many do. But too many don't.) We are taught to "Be hospitable to one another without grumbling" (1 Peter 4:9). Could your hospitality toward other Christians be described as abounding?

Bible study and prayer

God speaks to us through the Bible (2 Timothy 3:16-17). We talk to Him in prayer (Hebrews 4:16). Both are essential to proper spiritual growth and development. Some do little of either. How about you? Are you abounding in Bible study and prayer?

Can you list some other examples?

_____
_____
_____
_____

"And whatever you do, do it heartily, as to the Lord and not to men, knowing that from the Lord you will receive the reward of the inheritance; for you serve the Lord Christ" (Colossians 3:23-24).

Lesson 12

Perseverance

There are several words that are used interchangeably in the Bible—perseverance, patience, endurance, longsuffering and steadfastness.

Patience is defined in the dictionary as "perseverance in performing a task; endurance without complaining." It is the character quality that enables us to wait calmly for a desired result, to never give up in our devotion to God, to "keep on keeping on."

Someone said, "You can do anything if you have patience. You can even carry water in a sieve, if you wait until it freezes."

Former United States President Calvin Coolidge said, "Nothing in the world can take the place of persistence. Talent will not; nothing is more common than unsuccessful men with talent. Genius will not; unrewarded genius is almost a proverb. Education will not; the world is full of educated derelicts. Persistence and determination alone are omnipotent."

Here are a few of God's words on the subject:

"I press toward the goal for the prize of the upward call of God in Christ Jesus" (Philippians 3:14).

"For this reason I also suffer these things; nevertheless I am not ashamed, for I know whom I have believed and am persuaded that He is able to keep what I have committed to Him until that day" (2 Timothy 1:12).

"Therefore, my beloved brethren, be steadfast, immovable, always abounding in the work of the

> And let us **not grow weary** while doing good, for in due season we shall reap if we **do not lose heart**.
> - Galatians 6:9

> Let us **hold fast** the confession of our hope **without wavering**, for He who promised is faithful.
> - Hebrews 10:23

Lord, knowing that your labor is not in vain in the Lord" (1 Corinthians 15:58).

Bible Examples

Explain how each of these Bible characters displayed perseverance in their lives and find a passage or two to prove your point.

Noah _____
_____
_____

Joseph _____
_____
_____

Moses _____
_____
_____

Job _____
_____

Patience Versus an Explosive Temper

List verses for each of your answers.

1. Is anger wrong? _____
   _____
   _____

2. What about wrath? _____
   _____
   _____

3. What about being quick tempered? _____
   _____
   _____

Honest Self-Examination Time

What kinds of things make you impatient with people or situations?

_____
_____
_____
_____
_____
_____
_____

LESSON 12 Perseverance

Endurance in Hebrews

Explain how each of these passages from the book of Hebrews deals with our need for endurance.

3:6 _____
_____

4:1 _____
_____
_____

4:9-11 _____
_____
_____

6:11-12 _____
_____

10:23 _____
_____
_____

10:36-39 _____
_____
_____

12:1-2 _____
_____
_____

Galatians 6:9

1. What are some things that have discouraged you spiritually in the past?_____
_____
_____

Two Final Verses

My brethren, count it all joy when you fall into various trials, knowing that the testing of your faith produces **patience**. But let patience have its perfect work, that you may be perfect and complete, lacking nothing.

- James 1:2-4

Therefore, having been justified by faith, we have peace with God through our Lord Jesus Christ, through whom also we have access by faith into this grace in which we stand, and rejoice in hope of the glory of God. And not only that, but we also glory in tribulations, knowing that **tribulation produces perseverance; and perseverance, character; and character, hope**.

- Romans 5:1-4

2. Why does this verse say we shouldn't give up? _____
   _____

3. How do you overcome discouragement in your life? Give some practical suggestions you can share with the class. _____
   _____
   _____
   _____

At What Point Would You Have Quit?

Read 2 Corinthians 11:23-29

1. Which of these trials of Paul do you think would have been the worst?
   _____
   _____

2. Is there any one (or more) of these that would have made you say, "That's it; I've had enough"? _____
   _____

www.ingramcontent.com/pod-product-compliance
Lightning Source LLC
Chambersburg PA
CBHW070452050426
42451CB00015B/3447